PRACTICING SELF-LOVE

Proven Strategies For Loving Yourself"

YEMISI DANIELS

Table of Contents

Copyright Page

For more information, please contact:

Yemisi Daniels

yemregal@gmail.com **(+447862343230)**

Dedication

I dedicate this powerful book to God Almighty, who made it possible for me to write.

I also dedicate it to the blessed memory of my amazing Dad, Pa (Hon) Daniel Adeyeye Adeeko, who instilled in me the principles of self-love from an early age.

Even when life became tough and I almost lost myself, the foundation he gave me continually reinforced those principles, helping me regain my strength time and time again.

Acknowledgement

I wish to appreciate Dr. Ope Banwo of the F4L initiative, who anchored the Digital Skills Course, where for the first time in my life, I was able to identify my niche, during the bootcamp, to the actual course. It was as if the penny dropped, at that moment! This led to the birthing of my YouTube Channel, and the writing of this book, both on Self-love.

I am deeply grateful to my incredible friend, Dr. Yemisi Shode, and her wonderful husband for creating such a warm and inspiring environment that allowed this book to come to life. Their unwavering support and constant encouragement lifted my spirit at every step of this journey. They are truly rare gems, and I am profoundly blessed to have them in my life!

I cannot forget another great friend of mine, Mrs. Joyce Nwidag, whose words of encouragement kept me going throughout the period of writing this book. You are simply awesome!

I also wish to acknowledge my very good sister and friend, Ms. Yetunde Odebiyi, for introducing me to F4L. Thank you so much, my Twin. I love you loads.

Furthermore, I wish to acknowledge Bishop Ibro Zion of F4L initiative, for reading through and doing all the necessary corrections, designing the cover, and for formatting the book. Words are just inadequate to express my profound gratitude for your hard work on this book. All your efforts are greatly appreciated!

My heartfelt appreciation goes to all my children and grandchildren who, for over a long period of time, had helped in bringing my ideas together, which eventually became the compilation of my autobiography. You remain my constant inspiration!

Thank you for everything you do. I love you all deeply.

Why I Wrote This Book

In every journey toward self-improvement and personal development, there is a profound need to understand and embrace oneself fully. This book, "Practicing Self-Love: Proven Strategies for Loving Yourself," emerges from a deep-seated desire to address a universal challenge - learning to love and value ourselves.

A Personal Journey to Self-Love

The impetus for writing this book stems from my own journey toward self-love. Like many, I faced struggles with self-doubt, insecurity, and the relentless pursuit of external validation. I realized that the path to a fulfilling and authentic life required a shift in how I perceived and treated myself. Through years of exploration, study, and personal growth, I discovered that self-love is not a destination but a continuous practice. It is a practice that can transform every aspect of our lives.

The Need for Actionable Strategies

While there is no shortage of literature on self-love, I observed a gap in resources that offer practical, actionable strategies. Many existing books provide valuable insights but often fall short in guiding readers on how to apply these concepts in their daily lives. My goal was to bridge this gap by offering a guide that not only explains the principles of self-love but also provides concrete techniques and exercises that readers can implement immediately. This book is designed to be both informative and actionable, providing readers with tools they can use to foster self-love in their everyday experiences.

Addressing Common Struggles

Through conversations with friends, clients, and readers, I have encountered common struggles related to self-love issues such as negative self-talk, difficulties in setting boundaries, and challenges in maintaining a self-care routine. I wanted to address these struggles directly, offering solutions and strategies that are both practical and effective. By sharing the techniques that have worked for me and many others, I hope to empower readers to overcome their own obstacles and cultivate a deeper sense of self-love.

Inspiration from Others

The insights and strategies in this book are not solely derived from my experiences but are also influenced by the wisdom and research of experts in the field of self-love, psychology, and personal development. I have drawn inspiration from leading thinkers and practitioners who have dedicated their lives to understanding and promoting self-love. This book serves as a synthesis of their valuable contributions and my own insights, creating a resource that is comprehensive and grounded in evidence-based practices.

A Commitment to Positive Change

Ultimately, my commitment to writing this book is driven by a desire to contribute to a more positive and compassionate world. Self-love is a foundation for healthy relationships, personal growth, and overall well-being. By sharing this book, I hope to inspire readers to embark on their own journey of self-discovery and self-acceptance, leading to a ripple effect of positive change in their lives and communities.

As you read this book, I encourage you to approach it not just as a source of information but as a call to action. The strategies and exercises are designed to be lived and experienced, not merely read. By integrating these practices into your life, you take an active role in cultivating self-love and fostering a more fulfilling existence.

Thank you for joining me on this journey. It is my hope that this book serves as a guiding light in your path to self-love, offering support, inspiration, and practical tools to help you realize your fullest potential.

Introduction

What Is Self-Love?

Self-love is a concept that, at its core, seems simple yet holds immense depth and complexity. It transcends the superficial notion of merely liking oneself or indulging in fleeting pleasures. Rather, self-love is a profound and enduring commitment to recognising your own worth, treating yourself with kindness and compassion, and prioritising your well-being in a world that often encourages self-neglect. It is the foundation upon which a healthy, fulfilling, and resilient life is built.

Self-love is not a destination but a journey - a dynamic and evolving process that requires continual practice and reflection. It is about accepting yourself fully, flaws and all, and understanding that you deserve care, respect, and happiness simply because you exist. At its essence, self-love is the recognition that you are inherently valuable and worthy of love, independent of external achievements, validation, or approval.

Definition and Importance

To define self-love is to understand it as the deliberate act of caring for your own needs, nurturing your own growth, and acknowledging your intrinsic value. It involves a balanced relationship with oneself, where you honour your feelings, respect your boundaries, and actively cultivate a life that supports your well-being. Self-love is not self-indulgence or selfishness; it is the practice of making choices that prioritise your mental, emotional, and physical health.

The importance of self-love cannot be overstated. In a world rife with expectations, judgments, and constant comparisons, self-love serves as a protective shield against the detrimental effects of external pressures. It is the anchor that keeps you grounded when life becomes overwhelming, and the light that guides you through the darkest times. Without self-love, one is more susceptible to burnout, low self-esteem, unhealthy relationships, and a host of other challenges that can erode the quality of life.

The Difference Between Self-Love and Narcissism

A common misconception is that self-love is akin to narcissism, a distorted view that can deter individuals from embracing this vital practice. However, self-love and narcissism are fundamentally different. Narcissism is characterised by an inflated sense of self-importance, a lack of empathy, and a deep need for admiration and validation from others. It often masks a fragile self-esteem, with the narcissist's outward confidence hiding inner insecurities and fears.

In contrast, self-love is rooted in genuine self-respect and a healthy sense of self-worth. It does not seek to elevate oneself above others but rather fosters an inner harmony that allows one to interact with the world from a place of confidence and compassion. Where narcissism isolates, self-love connects - both with oneself and with others in a meaningful and authentic way. Self-love encourages empathy, kindness, and an understanding that loving oneself does not diminish the capacity to love others, but rather enhances it.

Why Self-Love Is Crucial for Overall Health and Well-being

The significance of self-love in overall health and well-being is profound. It is intimately linked to every aspect of your life - mental, emotional, and physical. When you practice self-love, you are more likely to engage in behaviours that promote health, such as eating well, exercising, and managing stress effectively. You are also more resilient in the face of adversity, better able to navigate life's challenges without succumbing to despair or self-doubt.

Emotionally, self-love fosters a sense of stability and inner peace. It allows you to acknowledge and process your feelings without judgment, reducing the likelihood of anxiety, depression, and other emotional disturbances. When you love yourself, you create a safe space within your own mind where you can retreat and recharge, free from the harsh criticisms that often come from both internal and external sources.

Mentally, self-love enhances your cognitive functions, such as focus, creativity, and problem-solving. By reducing the mental clutter associated with self-criticism and insecurity, you can approach tasks and challenges with clarity and confidence. This mental clarity not only improves your day-to-day productivity but also contributes to a more positive and hopeful outlook on life.

Physically, self-love translates into caring for your body as the vessel that carries you through life. It involves making choices that prioritize your health, such as getting enough rest, staying active, and listening to your body's needs. A strong sense of self-love encourages you to take care of your physical self, not out of vanity or obligation, but out of a deep respect and appreciation for your body's abilities and limitations.

In essence, self-love is the cornerstone of a healthy, balanced life. It is the practice that underpins every other aspect of well-being, ensuring that you are equipped to handle life's ups and downs with grace, resilience, and a sense of self-worth that remains unshaken by external circumstances.

The Journey to Self-Love

Embarking on the journey to self-love is a deeply personal and often transformative process. It requires patience, persistence, and a willingness to confront the inner narratives that have shaped your self-perception. This journey is not about perfection, but about progress - about taking small, consistent steps towards a more loving and accepting relationship with yourself.

The path to self-love often begins with self-awareness. Understanding your current relationship with yourself - how you think about yourself, how you treat yourself, and how you prioritize your needs - is the first step. From there, it involves unlearning harmful patterns, challenging negative self-beliefs, and replacing them with positive, affirming practices.

This journey is also about forgiveness - letting go of past mistakes and learning to embrace your imperfections as part of what makes you human. It is about cultivating self-compassion, giving yourself the same kindness and understanding that you would offer to a loved one. Over time, these practices become the building blocks of self-love, creating a foundation that supports your overall well-being and happiness.

Common Barriers to Self-Love

Despite its importance, self-love can be challenging to cultivate, often because of deep-seated barriers that stand in the way. One of the most significant barriers is negative self-talk, which can stem from childhood experiences, societal pressures, or past traumas. This inner critic can be relentless, convincing you that you are not worthy of love or respect.

Another common barrier is the fear of being perceived as selfish or arrogant. Many people, particularly those who have been taught to prioritize others over themselves, struggle with the idea of putting their own needs first. This can lead to a cycle of self-neglect, where one's own well-being is consistently sacrificed for the sake of others.

External influences, such as societal standards and cultural norms, also play a significant role in undermining self-love. In a world that often values appearance, success, and material wealth above all else, it can be difficult to maintain a sense of self-worth that is independent of external validation.

These barriers, while formidable, are not insurmountable. By recognizing and addressing them, you can begin to dismantle the obstacles that prevent you from fully embracing self-love.

The Emotional and Physical Benefits of Loving Yourself

Loving yourself has profound emotional and physical benefits that extend far beyond a mere sense of well-being. Emotionally, self-love acts as a buffer against the stresses and strains of daily life. It enhances your emotional resilience, enabling you to bounce back more quickly from setbacks and disappointments. With self-love, you are better equipped to handle criticism, rejection, and failure, viewing these experiences not as reflections of your worth, but as opportunities for growth and learning.

Self-love also fosters a greater sense of inner peace and contentment. When you accept and love yourself as you are, you free yourself from the constant need for external validation and approval. This self-acceptance allows you to live more authentically, making choices that align with your true values and desires, rather than conforming to the expectations of others.

Physically, self-love leads to healthier lifestyle choices. When you value yourself, you are more likely to engage in behaviours that support your health, such as eating nutritious foods, exercising regularly, and getting enough sleep. You are also more likely to seek medical care when needed and to listen to your body's signals, rather than pushing yourself to the point of burnout.

In summary, the emotional and physical benefits of self-love are far-reaching, impacting every aspect of your life. By cultivating self-love, you create a foundation for a healthier, happier, and more fulfilling life.

How to Use This Book

This book is designed to be a comprehensive guide on your journey to self-love, providing you with the tools, strategies, and insights needed to cultivate a deeper and more meaningful relationship with yourself. Each chapter builds on the previous one, guiding you step by step through the process of understanding, practicing, and sustaining self-love.

You may choose to read this book cover to cover, or you might prefer to focus on specific chapters that resonate with your current needs. Either way, the exercises, reflections, and actionable steps provided throughout are intended to help you integrate the principles of self-love into your daily life.

As you work through this book, remember that the journey to self-love is unique for each person.

There is no right or wrong way to approach it, and progress may come in waves rather than in a straight line. Be patient with yourself and allow the process to unfold naturally. With time, dedication, and practice, you will find that self-love becomes an integral part of your life, enhancing your overall health and well-being in ways you never thought possible.

Part 1: Understanding the Foundations of Self-Love

Self-love is often misunderstood as a vague concept, but its foundations are deeply rooted in psychological, emotional, and social constructs that shape how we see ourselves and interact with the world. To build a strong practice of self-love, it's essential to first understand these foundational elements- how they are formed, how they affect our behaviour and decisions, and how we can begin to reshape them in a way that fosters a healthier, more loving relationship with ourselves.

Chapter 1

The Psychology of Self-Love

To truly grasp the concept of self-love, it's crucial to first understand the psychology behind it. Many people unknowingly harbor self-hatred, constantly seeing themselves in a negative light. They struggle to find anything good within themselves, and as a result, they often experience the harshest challenges in life. This negative self-perception becomes a self-fulfilling prophecy, shaping not only how they view the world but also how the world responds to them.

How you view yourself is directly reflected in how others treat you. When you lack self-love, it can manifest in low self-esteem, self-doubt, and unhealthy relationships. People who don't love themselves often allow others to treat them poorly, accepting behavior they don't deserve because they don't believe they are worthy of better.

Practicing self-love is essential because it sets the standard for how others will love and respect you. By valuing yourself, you project confidence and worth, which invites others to treat you with the same level of respect and care. Self-love isn't selfish, it's the foundation for building healthier, more fulfilling relationships and creating a life that aligns with your true value.

When you prioritize self-love, you not only change your inner world, but you also shift how the external world responds to you.

1.1 The Role of Self-Esteem in Self-Love

Self-esteem is the foundation upon which self-love is built. It reflects how we perceive our worth and value, deeply affecting our capacity to care for ourselves. From early childhood, self-esteem is shaped by our environment by interactions with parents, teachers, peers, and later, colleagues and partners. Encouragement, a sense of belonging, and personal achievements help cultivate healthy self-esteem, while constant criticism, rejection, or failure can damage it.

When self-esteem is low, self-love becomes a challenge. Individuals may struggle to see themselves as deserving of care, leading to harmful patterns such as self-sabotage, seeking validation from others, and neglecting personal needs. These destructive cycles often prevent meaningful growth and happiness. Rebuilding self-esteem is essential for cultivating a healthy relationship with oneself.

The process involves recognizing where self-esteem was undermined, acknowledging its influence on thoughts and behaviors, and taking deliberate steps to strengthen it. By improving self-esteem, a strong foundation for self-love is established.

1.2 How Early Experiences Shape Self-Love

Early experiences, especially those from childhood, are powerful in shaping our capacity for self-love. The quality of our interactions with caregivers and the emotional environment we grew up in significantly affect how we view ourselves. If children are nurtured, supported, and encouraged, they are more likely to develop a positive self-concept and, eventually, a strong sense of self-love.

However, when children experience neglect, constant criticism, or abuse, their sense of self-worth can become compromised. These early wounds often carry into adulthood, manifesting as insecurity, self-doubt, or difficulty in maintaining healthy relationships. The psychology of attachment helps explain this: a secure attachment fosters confidence and self-love, while insecure attachment breeds emotional struggles. Healing from these early experiences requires acknowledging past pain, reprocessing those memories, and actively creating healthier emotional patterns in adulthood. The journey toward self-love often begins with understanding and healing from childhood wounds.

1.3 Understanding Self-Worth and Its Impact on Your Life

Self-worth refers to the inherent value you assign to yourself, independent of external factors such as success, appearance, or approval from others. Unlike self-esteem, which is often influenced by external validation, self-worth is rooted in the belief that you are enough simply by being who you are. This understanding of your intrinsic value provides the bedrock for self-love.

Unfortunately, societal and cultural pressures often distort our perception of self-worth. In a world that frequently ties worth to accomplishments, status, or material possessions, it can be difficult to maintain a healthy sense of self-worth. The risk of basing self-worth on these external metrics is that it becomes fragile crumbling in the face of failure, rejection, or comparison.

Reclaiming self-worth involves separating your value from these external markers and affirming your worth based on your inherent qualities. Practical steps to strengthen self-worth include practicing self-acceptance, challenging limiting beliefs, and focusing on internal values such as kindness, resilience, and authenticity. When self-worth is intact, it becomes easier to love and care for yourself without relying on external validation. By nurturing self-worth, you create a stable and enduring foundation for self-love.

Chapter 2

Identifying and Overcoming Negative Self-Talk

You cannot speak negatively and expect positive outcomes in your life. Your words have incredible power to shape the reality around you. When you constantly engage in negative talk, whether it's about yourself, your circumstances, or others, you unconsciously attract more negativity into your life. The mind absorbs what you tell it, and over time, those negative thoughts and words become self-fulfilling.

To experience peace and positivity, you must break free from the cycle of negativity. It starts by consciously choosing to speak words that uplift, encourage, and inspire. By shifting your inner dialogue and the words you express outwardly, you set the tone for a more harmonious and fulfilling life. Avoiding negativity is essential for creating an environment of solace, where your thoughts and words align with the positive experiences you wish to manifest.

2.1 Recognizing Self-Criticism and Limiting Beliefs

Negative self-talk is that harsh inner voice that constantly criticizes and diminishes you. It often echoes the judgments of others or societal pressures that suggest you're not enough. This self-criticism can be subtle or overt, but its effects are profound, slowly wearing down your confidence and sabotaging your self-worth.

The first step to overcoming this harmful pattern is recognizing it. Self-criticism can be deeply ingrained, appearing so natural that you might not even notice when it's happening. These thoughts may manifest as limiting beliefs, such as "I'm not smart enough," "I always fail," or "I don't deserve happiness." These beliefs act as mental barriers, blocking you from embracing self-love and limiting your potential.

By becoming aware of these negative patterns, you open the door to change. Self-awareness allows you to break free from the automatic loops of criticism and self-doubt. Once you begin to recognize the harsh, limiting beliefs that fuel negative self-talk, you can start dismantling them and replacing them with healthier perspectives.

2.2 Techniques to Challenge and Reframe Negative Thoughts

Identifying negative self-talk is just the beginning; the next critical step is to actively challenge and reframe those thoughts. It's not enough to simply notice when you're being self-critical, you need to question the validity of those thoughts and rework them into more balanced, supportive ones.

Cognitive-behavioral techniques (CBT) are particularly effective in this process. One of the main methods, cognitive restructuring, involves catching your negative thoughts, analyzing their logic, and replacing them with realistic, empowering alternatives. For instance, if you catch yourself thinking, "I always mess things up," you could reframe it into, "I've made mistakes before, but I've also learned and grown from them."

Mindfulness is another powerful tool. When you practice mindfulness, you observe your thoughts without judgment, creating a mental distance that allows you to disengage from negative patterns. This practice helps you recognize that your thoughts are just thoughts but not truths that you must believe or act upon. Instead of allowing negative thoughts to control your emotions and behavior, mindfulness allows you to let them pass without attachment.

Incorporating self-compassion exercises also transforms negative self-talk. Rather than berating yourself when things go wrong, speak to yourself with kindness and understanding. Imagine how you would respond to a friend going through the same struggles. By treating yourself with the same care, you shift from being your harshest critic to being your own greatest supporter.

2.3 Building a Positive Inner Dialogue

Developing a positive inner dialogue is crucial for fostering self-love. It's not about denying challenges or painting over difficulties with superficial positivity. Instead, it's about consciously choosing to speak to yourself in a way that uplifts, encourages, and nurtures your growth.

One way to build this positive inner dialogue is through affirmations - short, powerful statements that remind you of your value. These affirmations should resonate deeply and reflect the qualities you want to embody. For example, repeating statements like, "I am worthy of love," or "I trust myself to make wise decisions," can gradually reshape how you see yourself.

Journaling is another effective method. Writing down your thoughts helps clarify and externalize the inner dialogue you've been carrying around. By journaling about your struggles, victories, and goals, you can shift from ruminating on negativity to consciously focusing on progress and self-compassion.

The more you practice positive self-talk, the more natural it becomes. Over time, you'll find that the voice in your head is no longer your harshest critic, but your greatest advocate. This transformation in your inner dialogue strengthens your self-love and enhances your overall well-being, creating a foundation for deeper self-acceptance and growth.

Chapter 3

The Impact of Society and Culture on Self-Love

In Society and culture have an undeniable influence on the way we view ourselves, often shaping our self-worth and perception of what it means to be valuable or successful. From childhood through adulthood, we are surrounded by messages that tell us how we should look, act, and even feel.

These messages, if left unchecked, can erode our sense of individuality and make it harder to practice genuine self-love. To cultivate self-love in a world that often promotes unattainable ideals, we must become aware of these external influences and consciously work to counteract them.

3.1 Media Influence on Self-Perception

In the digital age, media exerts a powerful and pervasive influence on our sense of self. From television shows and advertisements to the carefully curated images on social media, we are constantly bombarded with portrayals of idealized lifestyles, bodies, and successes. The media often glorifies a narrow definition of beauty youth, thinness, flawless skin, and wealth which can lead people to feel inadequate or inferior if they don't fit into these narrowly defined boxes.

For example, on platforms like Instagram or TikTok, influencers often showcase perfect moments from their lives, luxurious vacations, fit bodies, and perfectly styled outfits. What we don't see are the less glamorous realities: the filters, editing, and hours of preparation behind those seemingly effortless images. Constant exposure to these "perfect" lives can distort our own self-image, making us believe that we are somehow less successful, attractive, or worthy.

However, recognizing the influence of media on our self-perception is the first step in taking back control. When we begin to question the validity of the images and messages we consume, we can start to distance ourselves from the unrealistic standards they promote. Setting boundaries around media consumption, such as limiting time spent on social media or being selective about the content we follow, helps foster a healthier self-image. Instead of comparing ourselves to these unattainable ideals, we can focus on appreciating our own unique qualities and achievements.

3.2 Breaking Free from Unrealistic Standards

Societal standards of beauty, success, and happiness are often unattainable, yet they are presented as the benchmarks everyone should aspire to. Whether it's the expectation to have the "perfect" body, to achieve rapid career success, or to maintain a picture-perfect relationship, these standards can create a sense of perpetual inadequacy. The pressure to conform to these unrealistic ideals can lead to self-doubt, anxiety, and even depression, as we feel we are constantly falling short of the expectations placed on us.

Breaking free from these societal expectations is essential for cultivating self-love. This begins with understanding that many of the standards we are trying to meet are not only unrealistic but also arbitrary. For instance, the "ideal" body type has changed throughout history and across cultures, what is considered attractive today may not be tomorrow. Similarly, the definition of success varies greatly from person to person. For one individual, success might mean financial stability, while for another, it could mean having meaningful relationships or making a difference in their community.

The key to breaking free from these societal pressures is to define success, beauty, and happiness on your own terms. Ask yourself what truly matters to you. Is it living authentically, being kind to others, or pursuing a passion? By shifting your focus away from society's arbitrary benchmarks and toward your own values, you allow yourself to live in alignment with your true self. This realignment opens the door to self-love because you are no longer chasing someone else's version of happiness rather you are creating your own.

3.3 Embracing Individuality in a Conformist World

In a world that often values conformity over individuality, embracing your uniqueness is a profound act of self-love. Society tends to reward people who fit neatly into predefined roles or adhere to popular norms, whether in appearance, behavior, or career choices. However, true self-love is found not in trying to mold yourself to fit these roles but in celebrating what makes you different.

Your individuality, your quirks, passions, strengths, and even your flaws is what sets you apart from others and makes you special. Trying to conform to society's expectations can suppress these unique qualities, leading to a loss of identity and self-worth. By embracing your individuality, you give yourself permission to be fully who you are, without the need for external validation.

This can be a difficult process, especially in a world that encourages uniformity. It requires courage to stand out, to take pride in your differences, and to pursue your own path, even if it goes against the grain. But the rewards of doing so are immense. When you accept and love yourself for who you truly are, rather than who society tells you to be, you cultivate an unshakable sense of self-worth. This self-acceptance forms the foundation of genuine self-love, where your value is derived not from how well you conform to others' expectations but from your own inherent worth.

To embrace individuality in a conformist world, start by identifying the qualities that make you unique and valuable. Celebrate your strengths and acknowledge your imperfections without judgment. Surround yourself with people who support your authentic self and encourage you to be the best version of you, rather than trying to fit into a particular mold. By doing so, you will create an environment where self-love can flourish, nurtured by the understanding that you are enough just as you are.

Society and culture exert a significant influence on self-love, often in ways that can hinder our ability to fully embrace ourselves. However, by becoming aware of these external pressures whether from media, societal expectations, or cultural norms and consciously choosing to redefine success, beauty, and worth on our own terms, we can cultivate a deeper, more authentic self-love. Embracing our individuality in the face of societal pressure to conform is the ultimate act of self-acceptance, allowing us to live fully and confidently as our true selves.

Chapter 4

The Connection Between Self-Love and Mental Health

The intricate relationship between self-love and mental health is crucial to understanding overall well-being. Self-love encompasses a range of attitudes and behaviors that emphasize treating oneself with kindness, compassion, and respect. When individuals practice self-love, they create a solid foundation for mental health, fostering resilience, reducing stress, and nurturing emotional strength essential for navigating life's inevitable challenges.

4.1 How Self-Love Prevents Burnout and Stress

Burnout and chronic stress are increasingly common in our fast-paced, high-demand society. These conditions often stem from prolonged exposure to stressors be they professional, personal, or social leading to physical, emotional, and mental exhaustion. When self-love is lacking, individuals may find themselves neglecting their needs, prioritizing obligations over self-care, and ultimately pushing themselves beyond healthy limits.

Prioritizing self-love requires recognizing personal needs and establishing clear boundaries. This means learning to say no to excessive demands, setting aside time for rest and rejuvenation, and allowing oneself to step back and recharge when needed. Self-love entails being attuned to the signs of burnout, which can manifest as chronic fatigue, irritability, cynicism, and a sense of detachment from life.

Incorporating self-care practices into daily life is a key aspect of self-love that acts as a buffer against stress. Engaging in enjoyable activities, such as hobbies, exercise, or mindfulness practices, replenishes energy and fosters emotional well-being. Regular self-reflection can also help individuals assess their emotional state and adjust their routines accordingly. By actively choosing to prioritize personal well-being, individuals create a healthier perspective on life's demands, enabling them to maintain balance and avoid the destructive consequences of burnout.

4.2 The Role of Self-Compassion in Mental Well-being

Self-compassion is an integral part of self-love, embodying a kind and understanding approach toward oneself, especially during challenging times.

It involves treating oneself with the same compassion one would offer to a close friend or loved one. This practice encourages individuals to acknowledge their suffering without judgment, creating an internal environment that fosters healing and emotional growth.

The three primary components of self-compassion self-kindness, mindfulness, and a sense of common humanity work together to enhance mental well-being. Self-kindness involves being gentle with oneself, particularly during moments of failure or difficulty. Rather than resorting to harsh self-criticism, individuals can learn to offer themselves words of encouragement and support, facilitating emotional healing and fostering resilience.

Mindfulness is another crucial aspect of self-compassion, allowing individuals to observe their thoughts and emotions without becoming entangled in them. This non-judgmental awareness creates space to acknowledge both positive and negative experiences, enabling individuals to accept their feelings without suppression or exaggeration. By cultivating mindfulness, individuals can mitigate the intensity of negative emotions and develop a more balanced emotional state.

Embracing a sense of common humanity helps individuals understand that suffering and imperfection are universal experiences. Recognizing that others also face difficulties reduces feelings of isolation and alienation, allowing individuals to connect with their shared humanity. This perspective not only fosters self-love but also promotes empathy and compassion toward others.

Research has demonstrated that self-compassion significantly alleviates anxiety, depression, and other negative emotional states. By cultivating self-compassion, individuals can develop greater emotional resilience, equipping themselves to navigate life's challenges without succumbing to self-doubt or negative thought patterns.

4.3 Techniques to Foster Emotional Resilience

Emotional resilience is defined as the ability to bounce back from adversity, setbacks, and challenges. It is closely tied to self-love, as individuals who engage in self-loving practices are generally better equipped to handle life's ups and downs. Building emotional resilience involves a multifaceted approach that incorporates various techniques and strategies.

Mindfulness practices, such as meditation, yoga, and deep-breathing exercises, play a significant role in cultivating present-moment awareness. These practices help individuals develop the ability to observe their thoughts and emotions without becoming overwhelmed by them. By creating distance from negative experiences, individuals can gain clarity and perspective, ultimately leading to reduced stress and anxiety.

Cognitive-behavioral techniques are also instrumental in fostering emotional resilience. These strategies encourage individuals to identify and challenge distorted thinking patterns that contribute to negative emotions. By recognizing unhelpful thoughts and reframing them into more balanced and realistic perspectives, individuals can shift their emotional landscape from one of negativity to one of empowerment. This cognitive restructuring can significantly enhance overall mental well-being.

In addition to mindfulness and cognitive-behavioral techniques, fostering a growth mindset is crucial for emotional resilience. A growth mindset entails believing that abilities and intelligence can be developed through effort, learning, and perseverance. Embracing challenges as opportunities for growth, rather than as threats to one's self-worth, encourages individuals to approach difficulties with confidence and adaptability. This mindset not only enhances resilience but also promotes a greater sense of self-love, as individuals recognize their capacity for growth and improvement.

Establishing supportive social connections is another vital aspect of building emotional resilience. Engaging with friends, family, or support groups creates a network of understanding and encouragement, allowing individuals to share their experiences and feelings. These connections foster a sense of belonging, reinforcing the idea that one is not alone in facing challenges.

Understanding the foundations of self-love is essential for creating lasting mental well-being. By exploring the psychological, emotional, and societal factors that influence self-love, individuals can navigate the barriers that impede their ability to practice self-love effectively. Recognizing the interplay between self-love and mental health equips individuals to apply actionable strategies that enhance their overall well-being.

Through cultivating self-love, practicing self-compassion, and implementing techniques to foster emotional resilience, individuals pave the way for a healthier, more fulfilling life. The journey toward self-love is ongoing, but the rewards greater mental health, emotional strength, and a profound sense of inner peace are well worth the effort.

Part 2: Practical Strategies for Cultivating Self-Love

In the first part of this book, we explored the foundational aspects of self-love, providing you with an understanding of what self-love is, the psychological and emotional components involved, and the societal influences that can affect it. Now, it's time to shift focus from understanding to action. Part 2 is dedicated to practical, actionable strategies that you can implement in your daily life to cultivate and sustain self-love. These strategies are designed to be accessible, adaptable, and effective, helping you to integrate self-love into your everyday routine in a way that feels natural and rewarding.

Chapter 5

Building a Self-Love Routine

Building a self-love routine is a vital component of nurturing a healthy relationship with oneself. Just as we maintain routines for physical health such as exercising, eating well, or maintaining hygiene our mental and emotional well-being deserves consistent, intentional care. By embedding self-love practices into our daily lives, we can cultivate a positive self-image and resilience that can withstand life's inevitable challenges.

5.1 The Importance of Daily Practices

Daily practices serve as the foundation for self-love, transforming it from an abstract concept into a tangible reality. Establishing a self-love routine means dedicating time each day to prioritize your mental and emotional needs. Small, manageable actions like affirmations, gratitude journaling, and mindful self-reflection can have a profound impact over time.

Affirmations involve repeating positive statements that reinforce self-worth and counteract negative self-talk. This practice helps reshape limiting beliefs, fostering a mindset of self-acceptance. Gratitude journaling encourages individuals to reflect on what they appreciate about themselves and their lives, promoting a more positive outlook. Mindful self-reflection involves taking time to evaluate your feelings and experiences, allowing for greater self-awareness and understanding.

Creating a self-love routine does not require monumental changes; rather, it thrives on consistency. By committing to these daily practices, you build habits that naturally integrate self-love into your life, transforming how you perceive yourself and interact with the world around you. Over time, these small actions accumulate, creating a powerful reservoir of self-acceptance and inner strength.

5.2 Morning Rituals for Self-Love

The way you start your day sets the tone for everything that follows. Establishing a morning ritual focused on self-love can enhance your mindset, resilience, and overall well-being. Engaging in mindful practices during the morning can profoundly impact your emotional state throughout the day.

Mindfulness meditation serves as an excellent way to center yourself before the day's activities begin. By taking just a few minutes to focus on your breath and cultivate present-moment awareness, you can create a sense of calm and clarity. Yoga is another powerful morning practice that integrates physical movement with mindfulness, allowing you to connect your body and mind while promoting relaxation and self-awareness.

Affirmations can be woven into your morning routine, providing a positive start to your day. By stating empowering phrases, such as "I am worthy of love and happiness" or "I embrace my uniqueness," you create a mental framework that supports self-love. Additionally, setting daily intentions can help you navigate the day with purpose, ensuring that you remain aligned with your self-love goals.

Tailoring these morning rituals to suit your lifestyle is essential for their sustainability. Whether you prefer a quiet moment of meditation or a more active practice like yoga, finding what resonates with you allows you to incorporate self-love seamlessly into your mornings.

5.3 Evening Practices for Reflection and Rejuvenation

Just as the morning sets the stage for the day, the evening offers a crucial opportunity for reflection and rejuvenation. Evening practices serve to process the day's events, release negativity, and prepare your mind and body for restful sleep.

Reflective journaling is a powerful evening ritual that encourages you to evaluate your day and acknowledge your experiences. Writing about what went well, what you learned, and what you appreciate about yourself can foster a sense of closure and gratitude. Additionally, gratitude exercises such as listing three things you are thankful for reinforce a positive mindset, allowing you to shift focus away from self-criticism and toward appreciation.

Incorporating relaxation techniques, such as deep-breathing exercises, progressive muscle relaxation, or gentle stretching, can further enhance your evening routine. These practices help release tension accumulated throughout the day, promoting a sense of peace and calm. By intentionally winding down with self-love, you create an environment conducive to restful sleep, ensuring you wake up rejuvenated and ready to embrace a new day.

Incorporating both morning and evening rituals into your routine establishes a framework for self-love that surrounds you throughout the day. By nurturing yourself at both the start and end of each day, you create a holistic approach to self-love that fosters emotional resilience, inner peace, and a profound connection with yourself. The journey of self-love is ongoing, but the commitment to daily practices empowers you to cultivate a deep and lasting relationship with yourself

.

Chapter 6

The Power of Affirmations and Positive Self-Talk

The words we speak to ourselves have immense power in shaping our beliefs, emotions, and overall self-perception. Affirmations and positive self-talk are two of the most effective tools for cultivating self-love and building a resilient, confident mindset. Through intentional repetition and the reprogramming of negative internal dialogue, it is possible to shift from self-doubt to self-assurance.

This chapter delves into the importance of affirmations, the process of integrating them into daily life, and how to transform negative self-talk into a positive, supportive inner dialogue.

6.1 Crafting Effective Affirmations

Affirmations are deliberate, positive statements that reflect how you wish to think, feel, or behave. When crafted with intention and repeated consistently, they have the potential to reshape your beliefs about yourself and your life. The key to creating powerful affirmations lies in ensuring that they resonate deeply and are aligned with your values, goals, and current emotional state. For affirmations to work effectively, they need to be specific, relevant, and emotionally impactful.

To craft effective affirmations, begin by focusing on areas where you desire growth or change. Use present tense, framing each affirmation as if the desired outcome is already a reality. This helps your mind align with the belief that positive change is not only possible but already unfolding. For example, instead of saying, "I will be confident someday," you might say, "I am confident and embrace my strengths."

Affirmations should also be framed in positive language. Avoid negations, such as "I am not afraid," and instead, focus on the outcome you want: "I am courageous and face challenges with strength." Emotional resonance is equally important. Phrases that evoke a deep sense of belief and empowerment will be more effective in reshaping your thought patterns.

Tailor affirmations to specific aspects of self-love, such as self-acceptance, self-care, or self-respect. Examples might include: "I accept myself fully, just as I am," or "I deserve to take time for self-care and nourishment." The more personal and relevant your affirmations, the more impactful they will be in your journey toward self-love.

6.2 Integrating Affirmations into Your Daily Life

Affirmations gain their true power through repetition and integration into daily life. It's not enough to write them down once or say them occasionally; affirmations must become a consistent part of your routine to influence your mindset effectively.

Start by identifying moments in your day where affirmations can naturally fit in. These could be during your morning routine, before a meeting, while exercising, or just before bed. The key is to find a rhythm that works for you so that these positive statements become second nature. Repeating affirmations during meditation can deepen their impact by combining the power of focused intention with relaxation and mindfulness.

Visual reminders can also help reinforce affirmations. Write them on sticky notes and place them in visible locations—your bathroom mirror, desk, or car dashboard. You could also keep a journal where you write down affirmations daily, turning them into a form of self-reflection. The act of writing itself reinforces the statement, embedding it further into your consciousness.

Technology offers another tool for integrating affirmations into your daily life. Apps designed for affirmations can send reminders throughout the day, providing prompts to repeat or reflect on positive statements. Setting phone alarms with affirmation notifications or using virtual post-it notes on your computer can ensure that affirmations are a regular part of your day, even in a busy schedule. Consistency is key, as the repetition of affirmations gradually reshapes your thought patterns, creating a mindset rooted in self-love and positivity.

6.3 Transforming Negative Self-Talk into Positive Dialogue

Negative self-talk is often a deeply ingrained habit, rooted in societal expectations, past experiences, or internalized criticism. This internal dialogue can manifest as self-doubt, harsh criticism, or feelings of inadequacy, undermining your self-worth and inhibiting your capacity for self-love. Transforming this negative self-talk into positive dialogue is a crucial step in building a healthier relationship with yourself.

The first step in this transformation is becoming aware of your inner dialogue. Pay attention to the thoughts that arise when you're faced with challenges, mistakes, or disappointments. Notice the tone of your self-talk whether it's supportive or critical. By recognizing negative patterns, you gain the power to challenge and change them.

Cognitive restructuring is an effective technique for reframing negative thoughts. This involves identifying irrational or unhelpful beliefs, challenging their validity, and replacing them with more balanced, realistic alternatives. For example, if your internal dialogue says, "I always fail," you can counter this by acknowledging past successes and reminding yourself that failure is a natural part of growth. Replacing that thought with a statement like, "I am learning and growing with each experience," shifts the focus from criticism to progress.

Another technique is thought-stopping, where you consciously interrupt negative thoughts as they arise. When a negative thought enters your mind, mentally say "stop" and immediately replace it with a positive affirmation. Over time, this practice weakens the hold of negative self-talk and strengthens positive self-perceptions.

Exercises such as journaling or mindfulness meditation can also support the process of transforming your internal dialogue. Journaling allows you to externalize your thoughts, making it easier to identify patterns and challenge negativity. Mindfulness meditation helps cultivate awareness of your thoughts without judgment, creating space to shift from criticism to compassion.

By actively transforming your inner dialogue, you foster a mindset that supports self-love and emotional well-being. Positive self-talk becomes a powerful tool, not only for countering negativity but for reinforcing the belief that you are worthy of love, respect, and kindness both from others and, most importantly, from yourself.

Incorporating affirmations and positive self-talk into your daily life builds the foundation for lasting self-love. These practices help reframe your mindset, turning negative beliefs into empowering truths that nurture your emotional and mental well-being.

Chapter 7

Cultivating Self-Compassion

Self-compassion is the foundation of a kind and supportive relationship with yourself. It is the ability to treat yourself with the same empathy and understanding that you would extend to others, especially in times of hardship. Unlike self-esteem, which fluctuates with success and failure, self-compassion is a steady, unshakeable source of emotional strength that remains constant even when things don't go as planned. Embracing self-compassion means accepting your imperfections and offering yourself care and kindness without judgment.

7.1 Understanding Self-Compassion and Its Benefits

At its core, self-compassion is about extending warmth and understanding to yourself, particularly during moments of failure, rejection, or difficulty. It involves recognizing your pain, responding to it with kindness, and avoiding harsh self-criticism. Instead of berating yourself when you fall short of expectations, self-compassion allows you to acknowledge your humanity and treat yourself with gentle care.

Three key elements make up self-compassion:

- **Self-kindness**: This means being gentle and supportive with yourself, especially when things don't go as expected. Instead of criticizing yourself for perceived failures, self-kindness encourages a more compassionate and understanding response. It's about offering yourself the same kind words and gestures you would offer a close friend.
- **Common humanity**: Recognizing that everyone experiences pain, failure, and disappointment helps to break the isolation

that often accompanies self-criticism. When you understand that suffering is part of the shared human experience, you are less likely to feel alone or inadequate. You become more capable of responding to your struggles with empathy and perspective.

- **Mindfulness**: Mindfulness is the practice of staying present and aware of your emotions without over-identifying with them or suppressing them. It allows you to observe your thoughts and feelings objectively, creating space for compassion. Rather than avoiding painful emotions or dwelling on them, mindfulness helps you acknowledge your suffering in a balanced and non-judgmental way.

Self-compassion is not about excusing mistakes or being complacent. It's about creating an inner environment of support that allows you to grow, heal, and move forward from difficult experiences with resilience. Research shows that people who practice self-compassion are more emotionally stable, experience less anxiety and depression, and have better overall mental well-being. They also tend to be more motivated to improve, as they approach challenges with a growth-oriented mindset rather than fear of failure.

7.2 Techniques for Practicing Self-Compassion

Developing self-compassion takes both practice and intentional effort. Here are some techniques that can help you cultivate a compassionate attitude towards yourself:

- **Loving-kindness meditation**: This meditation practice involves directing feelings of love and compassion towards yourself and others. You can start by repeating phrases such as "May I be happy, may I be healthy, may I be safe," focusing on generating feelings of warmth and kindness. Over time, this practice can help shift your internal dialogue towards a more compassionate tone.

- **Compassionate journaling**: Writing about your experiences with self-compassion can be incredibly healing. After a difficult day or experience, reflect on how you treated yourself. Did you criticize yourself, or were you kind and understanding? By acknowledging moments of self-judgment and rewriting them with a compassionate perspective, you can gradually change how you respond to challenging situations.

- **Self-soothing practices**: When you're feeling overwhelmed or upset, take steps to comfort yourself. This could be as simple as placing a hand on your heart and reminding yourself, "It's okay, I'm here for you." Self-soothing also involves doing things that bring you comfort, like taking a warm bath, listening to calming music, or engaging in activities that make you feel cared for.

When faced with challenges, practicing self-compassion helps you recover more quickly. For example, if you make a mistake at work or in a relationship, instead of beating yourself up, acknowledge that everyone makes mistakes and that this moment doesn't define you. By responding to your own pain with empathy, you cultivate resilience and emotional stability.

7.3 Overcoming Resistance to Self-Compassion

For many people, embracing self-compassion is difficult due to misconceptions about what it means. Some fear that being compassionate towards themselves will make them complacent or indulgent. Others may believe that self-criticism is necessary to stay motivated. These beliefs can create resistance to self-compassion, preventing people from experiencing its benefits.

One of the most common misconceptions is that self-compassion is a form of weakness or self-pity.

In reality, self-compassion requires strength and courage. It takes emotional maturity to face your suffering directly and respond to it with kindness. Far from making you weak, self-compassion actually builds emotional resilience, enabling you to handle life's difficulties with grace and understanding.

Another common barrier is the belief that being kind to yourself will make you less ambitious or driven. However, research shows that self-compassionate people are often more motivated to achieve their goals. Because they don't fear failure as much, they are more willing to take risks and embrace challenges. Self-compassion fosters a growth mindset, where mistakes are seen as opportunities for learning rather than proof of inadequacy.

To overcome resistance to self-compassion, it's helpful to reframe your understanding of it. Self-compassion is not about letting yourself off the hook or avoiding responsibility. It's about recognizing that you are human, that you will inevitably make mistakes, and that you deserve the same kindness and forgiveness that you extend to others. Instead of judging yourself harshly, offer yourself support so that you can learn, grow, and move forward more effectively.

By challenging misconceptions and practicing self-compassion, you can transform your relationship with yourself. You will develop a sense of inner strength, emotional balance, and self-acceptance that enhances every aspect of your well-being. Self-compassion empowers you to face life's challenges with resilience, knowing that you are deserving of love and care, no matter what.

Chapter 8

Setting Healthy Boundaries

Setting healthy boundaries is essential for preserving your well-being and cultivating a strong sense of self-love. Boundaries are not about shutting people out but about protecting your energy, time, and emotional health. They allow you to build respectful, fulfilling relationships with others while honoring your own needs and values. In this chapter, you will learn how to define, communicate, and manage your boundaries with clarity and confidence.

8.1 Understanding the Importance of Boundaries

Boundaries serve as a protective shield that helps you maintain balance and self-respect. Without them, it's easy to overextend yourself, say yes when you mean no, and allow others to drain your time and energy. Boundaries are crucial for maintaining healthy relationships both with others and with yourself.

There are different types of boundaries that play distinct roles in your life:

- **Emotional boundaries**: These involve protecting your emotional well-being by determining what you will and will not tolerate from others. They help prevent emotional manipulation, guilt-tripping, or being drawn into other people's drama.

- **Physical boundaries**: These define your comfort level with physical proximity, touch, and personal space. They ensure that your physical needs for safety and comfort are respected.

- **Psychological boundaries**: These are about protecting your thoughts, beliefs, and opinions from being dominated or dismissed by others. Psychological boundaries help you maintain your identity and stay true to your values, even in challenging situations.

By setting clear boundaries, you create an environment that fosters mutual respect, minimizes conflict, and enhances your self-worth. Boundaries are essential for preserving your energy, protecting your emotional health, and ensuring that your relationships are respectful and balanced.

8.2 How to Identify and Communicate Your Boundaries

Identifying your personal boundaries requires self-awareness and reflection. Start by considering the areas of your life where you feel drained, frustrated, or resentful. These emotions are often indicators that your boundaries are being ignored or violated. Ask yourself:

- Are there situations where I feel disrespected or taken advantage of?

- When do I feel overwhelmed or depleted by the demands of others?
- In what areas do I struggle to say no, even when I want to?

Once you've identified where your boundaries need reinforcement, the next step is to communicate them clearly and assertively. Effective communication of boundaries involves:

- **Using "I" statements**: Focus on your own needs and feelings without blaming others. For example, "I need some alone time to recharge" or "I'm not comfortable discussing that topic."
- **Being clear and direct**: Avoid vague or ambiguous language. Be specific about what you need and why it's important to you. For example, "I can't work late on Fridays because I need that time for family."
- **Remaining calm and respectful**: Assertiveness doesn't require aggression.

Communicating your boundaries in a calm and respectful manner makes it more likely that others will respond positively.

It's also important to remember that setting boundaries may feel uncomfortable at first, especially if you're not used to asserting your needs. However, with practice, it becomes easier, and the positive effects on your well-being will reinforce your commitment to maintaining those boundaries.

8.3 Managing Boundary Violations

Even with well-communicated boundaries, there will be times when others may attempt to push or ignore them. How you respond to these violations is key to maintaining your self-respect and reinforcing your boundaries.

Here are some strategies for managing boundary violations:

- **Gentle reminders**: Sometimes, people may unintentionally cross your boundaries, especially if they're not accustomed to you setting them. A simple reminder like, "Remember, I need that time for myself," can be enough to reinforce your limits without escalating the situation.

- **Being firm and assertive**: If someone repeatedly crosses your boundaries despite reminders, it's important to be more assertive. For example, "I've told you that I'm not available on weekends. I need you to respect that."

- **Enforcing consequences**: In some cases, you may need to establish consequences for continued boundary violations. This could mean distancing yourself from a relationship or declining further requests if your boundaries are consistently ignored.

- **Staying calm**: Managing boundary violations requires emotional control. If you become overly reactive, it can escalate conflict and undermine your efforts to set healthy limits. Remaining calm helps you maintain authority over your boundaries while addressing the issue with clarity.

Managing boundary violations can feel challenging, especially if you fear confrontation. However, responding calmly and assertively sends a clear message that your boundaries are non-negotiable. Over time, others will learn to respect your limits, and you'll experience greater self-respect and peace of mind.

By mastering the art of setting and enforcing boundaries, you reinforce your self-love and create an environment that values your well-being. Boundaries are not just about protecting yourself they are a way to cultivate relationships based on mutual respect and understanding, allowing you to live authentically and with confidence.

Chapter 9

Self-Care as an Act of Self-Love

Self-care is often misconstrued as a luxury or an occasional indulgence, but it is fundamentally a practice of self-love that supports your well-being on every level. By caring for your physical, emotional, mental, and spiritual health, you affirm your self-worth and cultivate a life grounded in balance and fulfillment. This chapter will guide you through the principles of effective self-care and how to make it an integral part of your everyday life.

9.1 The Pillars of Effective Self-Care

Effective self-care is about more than occasional relaxation or pampering it is a consistent practice that nurtures your entire being. To truly care for yourself, you must address your needs in a holistic way, attending to your physical, emotional, mental, and spiritual well-being. The key pillars of self-care include:

- **Physical Health**: This includes maintaining a balanced diet, getting regular exercise, and ensuring adequate rest. Taking care of your body is a foundation for overall well-being, as physical health directly impacts your mental and emotional state.

- **Emotional Well-Being**: Tending to your emotional health involves recognizing and honoring your feelings, setting healthy boundaries, and practicing self-compassion. This pillar emphasizes the importance of nurturing your emotional needs and processing your emotions in healthy ways.

- **Mental Clarity**: Maintaining mental health includes activities that help you focus, relax, and declutter your mind, such as mindfulness practices, journaling, or creative outlets. This pillar helps to reduce stress and anxiety, providing clarity and focus in daily life.

- **Spiritual Connection**: Whether through religious practices, meditation, or time spent in nature, nurturing your spiritual well-being is about connecting with something larger than yourself. It helps foster a sense of purpose and inner peace.

By understanding and balancing these pillars, you can create a self-care routine that holistically supports your health, happiness, and personal growth.

9.2 Developing a Personalized Self-Care Plan

Self-care is highly personal, and what works for one person may not work for another. To create a truly effective self-care routine, you need to develop a plan that fits your unique needs and lifestyle.

Start by assessing your current self-care habits. Are there areas where you feel overextended or neglected? Which pillars of self-care physical, emotional, mental, or spiritual need more attention? Reflecting on these questions will help you identify where to focus your efforts.

Once you've assessed your needs, you can begin crafting a self-care plan tailored to you. Consider these steps:

- **Set realistic goals**: Whether it's exercising more, spending time in nature, or scheduling regular downtime, create goals that are achievable and sustainable. Break them down into manageable steps to avoid feeling overwhelmed.

- **Incorporate self-care into your routine**: Use time management techniques to integrate self-care into your daily schedule. You can start with small changes, such as dedicating 10 minutes a day to meditation or scheduling a weekly phone call with a close friend.

- **Monitor and adjust**: Your self-care needs will change over time. Be flexible and adapt your plan as necessary to reflect life changes, stressors, or shifting priorities.

By developing a personalized self-care plan, you can make self-care a non-negotiable part of your life, fostering resilience and self-love on a daily basis.

9.3 Overcoming Common Obstacles to Self-Care

Despite the importance of self-care, many people struggle to maintain a consistent routine due to obstacles like time constraints, guilt, or misconceptions about self-care being selfish. This section will address these common barriers and provide strategies to overcome them.

- **Time constraints**: One of the biggest challenges is finding time for self-care in a busy schedule. To overcome this, prioritize self-care by treating it like any other important appointment. Plan it into your day, even if it's just a few minutes of quiet time or a brief walk outside.

- **Guilt**: Many people feel guilty for taking time for themselves, particularly if they are responsible for others. It's important to recognize that self-care is not selfish; in fact, taking care of yourself makes you better equipped to care for others.

- **Misconceptions**: Some people believe self-care is indulgent or unnecessary. However, self-care is essential for maintaining mental, emotional, and physical health. It's about preventing burnout, managing stress, and enhancing overall well-being.

By addressing these obstacles, you can shift your mindset to view self-care as a vital component of self-love and personal growth. With the right tools and strategies, maintaining a consistent self-care routine becomes much easier, allowing you to nurture yourself even amid life's demands.

Embracing self-care as an act of self-love is not just about improving your well-being, it's about sending a message to yourself that you are worthy of care, attention, and love. When you consistently practice self-care, you cultivate a deeper sense of self-respect and nurture the foundation of a healthy, fulfilling life.

Chapter 10

Nurturing Healthy Relationships

Building and maintaining healthy relationships is essential to personal growth and self-love. Relationships are a core part of our lives, and the ones we nurture can either elevate us or hold us back. Understanding how to cultivate supportive relationships, set boundaries, and walk away from toxic dynamics is critical for preserving your self-love and emotional well-being.

10.1 The Role of Supportive Relationships in Self-Love

Supportive relationships serve as a mirror for your self-worth. When you surround yourself with people who respect, value, and uplift you, it becomes easier to foster a sense of self-love. These relationships act as a foundation during tough times, offering encouragement and reminding you of your intrinsic value. In contrast, toxic relationships can erode self-confidence, perpetuate negative self-talk, and undermine your emotional health.

In this section, we'll explore:

- **What makes a relationship supportive**: At the heart of supportive relationships are qualities like respect, trust, open communication, and mutual care. These relationships create a safe space where you can be yourself without fear of judgment or rejection. You'll learn how to identify relationships that contribute positively to your self-esteem and align with your journey toward self-love.

- **The role of reciprocity**: Supportive relationships are built on the principle of reciprocity both giving and receiving care. Healthy dynamics are not one-sided; both parties contribute equally, ensuring emotional balance and mutual respect.

- **The dangers of toxic relationships**: Toxic relationships, on the other hand, often involve manipulation, control, or emotional abuse. These relationships sap your energy, foster feelings of inadequacy, and can cause long-term harm to your self-image. Recognizing these toxic traits is the first step in protecting yourself from their damaging effects.

By learning to identify and foster supportive relationships, you create an environment that nurtures self-love, personal growth, and emotional stability.

10.2 Building and Maintaining Boundaries in Relationships

Boundaries are the invisible lines that define your personal space, values, and emotional limits. They are essential for maintaining self-respect, protecting your well-being, and ensuring that your relationships are healthy and balanced. Without clear boundaries, relationships can become unbalanced, leading to feelings of resentment, burnout, or emotional exhaustion.

In this section, we will cover:

- **The importance of boundaries**: Boundaries are not about keeping people out but about ensuring that your needs, values, and emotional well-being are respected. Setting boundaries allows you to take control of your interactions, ensuring that your relationships remain healthy and supportive of your self-love journey.

- **How to identify your boundaries**: The first step in setting boundaries is recognizing your limits. Reflect on past experiences where you've felt uncomfortable, disrespected, or overwhelmed. These moments often signal areas where boundaries are needed. Understanding what makes you feel safe, respected, and valued will help you define your limits.

- **Communicating boundaries effectively**: Once you've identified your boundaries, the next step is communicating them clearly and assertively. You'll learn how to express your needs in a way that's both firm and respectful, ensuring that others understand where your limits lie. It's important to communicate these boundaries without fear of confrontation or guilt, as they are essential to your well-being.

- **Dealing with resistance**: Not everyone will respond positively to your boundaries. Some may resist, challenge, or even disregard them entirely. In these situations, it's crucial to stand firm and reaffirm your limits without succumbing to pressure. You'll explore strategies for handling resistance with confidence, ensuring that your boundaries are upheld without unnecessary conflict.

Setting and maintaining boundaries is an act of self-love. It reinforces your worth, protects your emotional energy, and ensures that your relationships are aligned with your values and needs.

10.3 Ending Toxic Relationships and Healing from Emotional Wounds

Sometimes, despite your best efforts, certain relationships cannot be salvaged. Toxic relationships, those that are emotionally abusive, manipulative, or consistently disrespectful—can take a heavy toll on your self-esteem and mental health. Recognizing when it's time to walk away is a crucial part of nurturing self-love and protecting your well-being.

In this section, you'll explore:

- **Recognizing when a relationship is toxic**: Toxic relationships often involve patterns of emotional manipulation, control, or neglect. You may feel constantly drained, anxious, or unworthy in these relationships. Identifying these red flags is the first step in making the difficult decision to end a toxic relationship.

- **The process of ending toxic relationships**: Ending a toxic relationship is never easy, but it's necessary for your emotional health. You'll learn how to navigate the complexities of this process, whether it involves having a difficult conversation or gradually distancing yourself. The key is to prioritize your well-being and recognize that letting go is an act of self-love.

- **Healing from emotional wounds**: After ending a toxic relationship, the healing process begins. Emotional wounds left by these relationships can run deep, affecting your self-worth and emotional stability. This section will offer practical steps for healing, including seeking therapy, practicing self-forgiveness, and engaging in consistent self-care routines.

- **Moving forward with self-love**: Healing from a toxic relationship isn't just about recovering from the past; it's about building a future where your relationships are healthier and more supportive. By focusing on self-compassion, you can rebuild your confidence, regain your sense of worth, and attract relationships that align with your values and emotional needs.

Recognizing the need to end a toxic relationship and taking steps to heal from the emotional damage are essential aspects of nurturing self-love. With time, patience, and self-compassion, you can move forward stronger and more confident, with relationships that truly support your well-being.

Chapter 11

Embracing Self-Acceptance

Self-acceptance is the foundation upon which true self-love is built. It involves recognizing and embracing all aspects of yourself, both the good and the not-so-good, without judgment or denial. While self-improvement is often the focus of personal growth, self-acceptance is about acknowledging where you are right now and finding peace with it.

When you fully accept yourself, you free yourself from the constant pressure of perfectionism, self-criticism, and comparison to others. This chapter explores how to embrace self-acceptance as a powerful tool for lasting self-love and emotional well-being.

11.1 The Power of Self-Acceptance

Self-acceptance is a liberating and transformative process that allows you to honor every part of yourself, your strengths, weaknesses, accomplishments, and failures. It's not about resigning yourself to flaws or giving up on self-improvement, but rather about making peace with who you are at any given moment. When you practice self-acceptance, you let go of the unrealistic expectation of perfection, recognizing that being human means having both light and shadow sides.

Here are some of the impacts of self-acceptance:

- **The impact of self-acceptance on mental and emotional well-being**: Self-acceptance has profound effects on your mental health. It reduces anxiety, depression, and stress, while boosting self-esteem and resilience. When you accept yourself, you are less likely to be swayed by external criticism or validation and more grounded in your inner sense of worth.

- **How self-acceptance fosters self-love**: At its core, self-love is about valuing and caring for yourself unconditionally. Self-acceptance is the pathway to this kind of love because it invites you to appreciate yourself without trying to change or "fix" anything. This, in turn, allows for a deeper and more sustainable self-love that isn't dependent on external achievements or approval.

- **Self-acceptance as a holistic practice**: True self-acceptance means embracing all aspects of your being physical, emotional, mental, and spiritual. It's not enough to accept certain parts of yourself while rejecting others. This section will guide you in recognizing and accepting your whole self, which is essential for inner peace and long-term happiness.

By embracing the power of self-acceptance, you cultivate a sense of inner calm and confidence, allowing you to navigate life's challenges from a place of self-love rather than self-criticism.

11.2 Strategies for Cultivating Self-Acceptance

Self-acceptance isn't something that happens overnight; it requires intentional practice and a shift in mindset. Many people struggle with accepting themselves due to deeply ingrained negative beliefs or societal pressures to conform to certain ideals. However, by applying practical strategies, you can begin to cultivate a deeper sense of self-acceptance and appreciation.

In this section, you'll explore:

- **Self-reflection exercises**: The first step toward self-acceptance is self-awareness. By engaging in regular self-reflection, you gain a clearer understanding of your thoughts, feelings, and behaviors. This section will introduce journaling exercises that help you reflect on your strengths and areas for growth without judgment, fostering a mindset of acceptance.

- **Gratitude practices**: Practicing gratitude for who you are, just as you are, can shift your focus from self-criticism to self-appreciation. By regularly acknowledging and expressing gratitude for your qualities, talents, and efforts, you can build a more positive relationship with yourself. This chapter will provide actionable tips for integrating gratitude practices into your daily routine.

- **Mindfulness techniques**: Mindfulness encourages you to stay present and observe your thoughts and emotions without judgment. By practicing mindfulness, you can become more aware of self-critical patterns and learn to replace them with self-compassion. This section will explore simple mindfulness exercises that help you stay grounded in self-acceptance.

- **Reframing negative self-perceptions**: Negative self-talk and limiting beliefs can be major barriers to self-acceptance. This section will teach you how to identify and challenge these negative perceptions, replacing them with affirming and realistic beliefs about yourself. By focusing on your positive qualities and past successes, you can create a more balanced and compassionate self-view.

Through these practical strategies, you'll learn how to cultivate self-acceptance in your daily life, making it a habit that strengthens your emotional resilience and fosters greater self-love.

11.3 Overcoming Self-Judgment and Embracing Imperfections

Self-judgment is one of the biggest obstacles to self-acceptance. We are often our own harshest critics, holding ourselves to impossible standards and punishing ourselves for perceived failures or flaws. However, self-judgment doesn't serve us, it only deepens feelings of inadequacy and shame. Learning to overcome self-judgment is a key component of embracing self-acceptance.

In this section, we'll address:

- **Sources of self-judgment**: Self-judgment can stem from various sources, including childhood experiences, societal expectations, or comparison to others. Understanding where your self-critical tendencies come from can help you begin to dismantle them. You'll learn to identify the roots of your self-judgment and begin the process of letting go of these harmful patterns.

- **Cognitive restructuring techniques**: Cognitive restructuring is a powerful tool for shifting negative thought patterns. This section will introduce techniques that help you recognize self-critical thoughts and replace them with more balanced and self-compassionate perspectives. By reframing how you think about your mistakes or shortcomings, you'll begin to embrace them as part of your human experience rather than as reasons for self-criticism.

- **Practicing self-compassion**: Self-compassion involves treating yourself with the same kindness, understanding, and support that you would offer to a friend. This section will provide exercises for cultivating self-compassion, including self-soothing techniques and compassionate self-talk. By practicing self-compassion, you can create a more forgiving and accepting relationship with yourself.

- **Embracing imperfections as part of self-acceptance**: No one is perfect, and embracing your imperfections is a vital step toward self-acceptance. This chapter will help you shift your perspective on flaws, viewing them not as defects but as natural parts of your unique human experience. By accepting your imperfections, you free yourself from the unrealistic expectation of perfection and open yourself up to a more authentic and loving relationship with yourself.

By overcoming self-judgment and embracing your imperfections, you can cultivate a more compassionate and forgiving relationship with yourself. This, in turn, deepens your sense of self-acceptance and allows you to live with greater peace and authenticity.

Chapter 12

Living Authentically

Living authentically is a vital part of self-love, as it requires a commitment to being true to who you are, regardless of societal pressures or external expectations. When you live authentically, you honor your inner self, stay aligned with your values, and express your true desires and emotions. Authenticity enhances self-confidence, builds self-trust, and fosters a life of integrity and fulfillment. This chapter delves into what it means to live authentically, how it strengthens your self-love, and provides practical guidance on how to achieve and maintain authenticity in your daily life.

12.1 The Importance of Authenticity in Self-Love

Authenticity is the cornerstone of self-love. At its essence, living authentically means having the courage to embrace who you truly are and showing up in the world as your genuine self. This involves expressing your thoughts, feelings, and beliefs without masking or diluting them to meet the expectations of others. When you live authentically, your self-worth is not tied to external validation, but rather grounded in your own sense of integrity and self-respect.

In this section, let us explore:

- **The connection between authenticity and self-love**: Authenticity is about honoring your true self, which naturally strengthens your relationship with yourself. When you live authentically, you create a life that reflects your values and passions, which in turn fosters a deeper sense of self-respect and love.

- **The benefits of living authentically**: Living authentically enhances your overall well-being. You experience greater self-confidence, fulfillment, and inner peace because you're no longer trying to conform to others' expectations. Authenticity reduces feelings of inadequacy and impostor syndrome, as it allows you to embrace your uniqueness without apology.

- **How authenticity empowers you to lead a more fulfilling life**: Authenticity frees you from the constraints of seeking approval or living up to unrealistic standards. By being true to yourself, you can focus on what truly matters to you, make decisions that align with your deepest values, and pursue meaningful goals. This not only enriches your life but also strengthens your self-love.

Living authentically is both liberating and empowering. It allows you to stand firmly in your truth, fostering a life that is not only true to your values but also a reflection of deep self-respect.

12.2 Identifying and Overcoming Barriers to Authenticity

Living authentically can be challenging due to the many internal and external barriers that prevent us from expressing our true selves. These barriers often stem from societal expectations, fear of judgment, and long-held beliefs that push us to conform rather than embrace our individuality. However, by recognizing and addressing these barriers, you can cultivate a more authentic and self-loving life.

Permit me to show you some few more things in this section like:

- **Common barriers to authenticity**: Many people struggle to live authentically due to external pressures, such as societal norms, cultural expectations, or fear of being judged. Internal barriers, such as self-doubt, fear of rejection, and limiting beliefs, can also prevent you from embracing your true self. This section will help you identify these obstacles and understand how they manifest in your life.

- **Overcoming fear of judgment**: Fear of judgment is a major hindrance to authenticity. Whether it's the fear of disappointing others or being seen as "different," this fear can cause you to hide parts of yourself or conform to the expectations of others. This chapter will guide you in developing resilience to external judgments by prioritizing your own opinion of yourself over the opinions of others.

- **Breaking free from societal pressures**: Society often dictates who we should be, how we should act, and what success looks like. These pressures can lead to a disconnect between your true self and the version of yourself that you present to the world. This section will explore how to break free from these societal expectations, encouraging you to align your life with your personal values rather than external standards.

- **Internal work to challenge limiting beliefs**: Limiting beliefs are deeply rooted thoughts that convince you that you aren't "good enough" or that you must change to be accepted. This section will teach you how to challenge these beliefs by replacing them with affirmations that align with your authentic self. By shifting your mindset, you'll be better equipped to live authentically and confidently.

By identifying and overcoming these barriers, you'll begin to align your actions and decisions with your true self. This alignment fosters deeper self-acceptance and strengthens your self-love, as you are no longer trying to be someone you're not.

12.3 Practices for Staying True to Yourself

Living authentically is an ongoing process that requires self-awareness, courage, and commitment. It's not always easy to stay true to yourself, especially in situations where your authenticity is challenged or when the pressure to conform feels overwhelming. However, with the right practices, you can maintain your authenticity even in the face of adversity.

In this section, let us explore:

- **Self-reflection as a tool for authenticity**: Regular self-reflection helps you stay in tune with your true values, desires, and emotions. This section will introduce reflective practices, such as journaling and meditation, that allow you to check in with yourself and ensure that your actions align with your authentic self.

- **Setting authentic goals**: Authenticity in goal-setting is about pursuing what truly matters to you, rather than chasing goals that are imposed by others or society. This section will guide you in setting goals that align with your core values and passions, helping you live a life that reflects your true self.

- **Navigating challenges to authenticity**: Life will present moments where being authentic is difficult—whether it's in a professional setting, social situation, or personal relationship. This section will offer strategies for handling these situations with grace and integrity, ensuring that you don't compromise your authenticity out of fear or pressure.

- **Practicing self-expression**: Authentic living involves expressing yourself fully and truthfully. Whether through words, actions, or creative outlets, self-expression allows you to showcase your true self to the world. This section will provide tips on embracing and practicing self-expression, both in everyday interactions and in more personal or creative endeavors.

- **Seeking feedback from trusted individuals**: Sometimes, the people closest to you can help you stay accountable to your authenticity. By seeking feedback from trusted friends or mentors, you can gain insights into areas where you may be straying from your true self or where you could embrace more authenticity. This practice helps you stay grounded in your self-love and authenticity.

By integrating these practices into your daily life, you'll be better equipped to live authentically and navigate the challenges that come with it. Authenticity fosters a deeper, more resilient form of self-love, as it requires you to honor your true self in every aspect of your life.

Chapter 13

Self-Love in Professional Life

Integrating self-love into your professional life is essential for achieving a sense of purpose, fulfillment, and balance. Many people spend a significant portion of their lives in the workplace, and it's vital that this time is aligned with your personal values, strengths, and goals. A career that fosters self-love not only supports your professional ambitions but also nurtures your emotional and mental well-being. In this chapter, you will explore how to infuse self-love into your career by setting goals that resonate with your true self, navigating challenges with confidence, and finding harmony between your work and personal life.

13.1 Setting Career Goals Aligned with Self-Love

Setting career goals that align with self-love means pursuing work that reflects who you truly are, including your values, strengths, and passions. Often, people chase career success defined by external standards, but self-love requires you to prioritize personal fulfillment over societal expectations. By crafting goals that honor your authentic self, you set the stage for a more rewarding and meaningful professional journey.

In this section, you'll learn how to:

- **Assess your current career satisfaction**: Self-love in your career begins with self-awareness. Take time to evaluate your current professional path and identify whether your job reflects your values, interests, and strengths. Are you passionate about your work? Do you feel fulfilled? By answering these questions, you can determine whether your current trajectory aligns with your self-love.

- **Identify areas for growth**: Self-love doesn't mean settling for less. It involves recognizing where you need to grow and improve while being kind to yourself in the process. Identify areas in your career where you can expand your skills, explore new opportunities, or take on challenges that excite you. Growth that is in line with your authentic self leads to personal and professional fulfillment.

- **Set authentic career goals**: Setting career goals that align with self-love is about creating a vision for your future that reflects your true aspirations, not just what is expected of you. This section will help you define professional objectives that resonate with your values, whether that means seeking more meaningful work, aiming for a leadership position, or transitioning to a new industry altogether. The key is to ensure that your career ambitions support your well-being and happiness.

- **Foster professional fulfillment and personal growth**: Aligning your career with self-love creates a professional life where personal growth and fulfillment are at the forefront. You'll learn how to balance ambition with well-being, ensuring that the pursuit of your goals doesn't come at the cost of your mental or emotional health.

By aligning your career goals with self-love, you cultivate a work life that not only supports your financial and professional success but also nourishes your inner self.

13.2 Navigating Workplace Challenges with Self-Love

The workplace can be a source of both fulfillment and stress. Navigating challenges at work requires a strong foundation of self-love, as it helps you remain grounded, assertive, and resilient even in difficult environments. Whether you face workplace conflicts, demanding workloads, or unsupportive colleagues, approaching these challenges with self-love enables you to protect your well-being and stay true to yourself.

In this section, you'll explore:

- **Assertive communication**: Speaking up for yourself in the workplace is an essential aspect of self-love. Whether it's advocating for your needs, setting boundaries with colleagues, or voicing your opinions in meetings, assertive communication helps you maintain self-respect. This chapter will offer strategies for effectively expressing yourself in a way that is confident, respectful, and aligned with your values.

- **Stress management techniques**: Work-related stress can erode your self-love if not managed properly. This section will provide techniques for managing stress in a healthy way, such as mindfulness practices, deep breathing exercises, and time management skills. You'll learn how to prioritize self-care, even in high-pressure environments, to avoid burnout and maintain your mental health.

- **Handling workplace conflicts**: Conflict is inevitable in any workplace, but how you handle it can make a significant difference in your well-being. This section will guide you in navigating workplace conflicts with grace and self-respect, whether it's addressing a disagreement with a colleague or managing difficult feedback from a supervisor. By approaching conflicts with self-love, you'll foster healthier professional relationships and preserve your emotional balance.

- **Maintaining self-respect in unsupportive environments**: Sometimes, you may find yourself in a work environment that challenges your self-worth, whether through toxic management, uncooperative colleagues, or unrealistic demands. This section will provide strategies for maintaining self-respect and emotional stability in such environments. You'll learn how to recognize when a situation is detrimental to your well-being and take steps to protect yourself, whether by setting boundaries, seeking support, or even considering a career change.

By navigating workplace challenges with self-love, you create a healthier and more sustainable work environment for yourself, ensuring that your career doesn't compromise your emotional or mental health.

13.3 Balancing Professional and Personal Life

Achieving a balance between your professional and personal life is crucial for maintaining self-love and overall well-being. Many people struggle with the demands of their careers spilling over into their personal lives, leaving little time for rest, self-care, or meaningful relationships. A balanced life allows you to pursue your career goals while still prioritizing your personal happiness and fulfillment.

In this section, you'll explore:

- **The importance of work-life balance**: Balancing work and personal life is essential for long-term success and happiness. When your professional life consumes all your energy, your personal well-being suffers. This section will help you recognize the signs of an imbalanced life and take steps to restore harmony between your career and personal pursuits.

- **Time management and prioritization**: Effective time management is key to achieving balance. This section will offer practical tips for managing your time in a way that allows you to meet your professional obligations without sacrificing personal time. You'll learn how to prioritize tasks, delegate when necessary, and create a schedule that supports both your career and your personal life.

- **Setting boundaries at work**: Boundaries are essential for maintaining a healthy work-life balance. This section will provide strategies for setting boundaries with colleagues, supervisors, and clients, ensuring that your personal time is respected. Whether it's limiting after-hours communication or setting realistic expectations for your availability, boundaries help you protect your personal life and maintain your self-love.

- **Prioritizing self-care**: In the hustle of professional life, self-care often falls by the wayside. However, nurturing your well-being is essential for long-term success. This section will emphasize the importance of self-care practices such as exercise, relaxation, hobbies, and time with loved ones, showing you how to incorporate these into your routine without feeling guilty or neglecting your career.

- **Creating a balanced schedule**: Achieving balance requires intentional scheduling that honors both your professional ambitions and personal needs. This section will guide you in creating a balanced schedule that allows time for work, rest, self-care, and meaningful relationships. By doing so, you'll enhance your overall satisfaction and ensure that neither your career nor personal life becomes overwhelming.

By achieving balance between your professional and personal life, you create a foundation for lasting self-love and well-being. A balanced life allows you to enjoy your work, nurture your relationships, and take care of yourself, leading to greater overall fulfillment.

Chapter 14

Self-Love and Personal Growth

Self-love and personal growth are intimately connected. When you prioritize self-love, you cultivate the self-awareness, confidence, and resilience needed to pursue your own development. Personal growth, in turn, strengthens your self-love, as you experience greater fulfillment and pride in the person you are becoming. In this chapter, we will explore how self-love serves as the foundation for personal growth and how embracing change and new challenges can lead to a more empowered and fulfilling life.

14.1 The Connection Between Self-Love and Personal Development

Self-love is not about stagnation; it's about nurturing a mindset that fosters curiosity, resilience, and a willingness to grow. By cultivating self-love, you develop the inner security needed to seek out new opportunities and challenges that lead to personal development.

In this section, let us look at:

- **How self-love fosters a growth mindset**: A growth mindset is the belief that your abilities, intelligence, and potential can develop with effort and learning. Self-love encourages this mindset because when you truly value yourself, you understand that you are always worthy of improvement. You're not afraid of failure or setbacks because you see them as part of the process of growth.

- **The importance of setting personal goals**: Self-love motivates you to set meaningful goals that align with your values and desires. Instead of striving for perfection or seeking approval from others, self-love leads you to pursue personal growth out of a desire to become the best version of yourself. This section will explore the connection between goal-setting and self-love, emphasizing how personal development flourishes when you're working toward goals that reflect your true self.

- **Embracing new experiences and lifelong learning**: Self-love opens you up to new possibilities and experiences that expand your knowledge and abilities. Whether it's learning a new skill, exploring a new hobby, or taking on a personal challenge, self-love encourages you to continuously seek opportunities for growth. This section will discuss how to adopt a mindset of lifelong learning and self-improvement, where growth is celebrated, and stagnation is avoided.

Self-love serves as a powerful foundation for personal development. By loving yourself, you create a safe space for growth, exploration, and change. You'll feel more confident to take risks, pursue new goals, and challenge yourself in ways that lead to a richer, more fulfilling life.

14.2 Setting Personal Growth Goals

Personal growth thrives when you have clear and actionable goals. Setting these goals is an essential step in your self-love journey, as it enables you to identify areas for improvement and create a plan for achieving your full potential. When your goals are aligned with self-love, they serve as a road map to a life that reflects your values, passions, and aspirations.

In this section, let us explore:

- **How to identify areas for personal growth**: Personal growth begins with self-awareness. This section will guide you in reflecting on your current strengths, challenges, and aspirations. You'll identify areas where you want to grow—whether it's building confidence, learning new skills, improving relationships, or enhancing your mental and emotional well-being.

- **The process of setting SMART goals**: Once you've identified areas for growth, the next step is setting goals that are Specific, Measurable, Achievable, Relevant, and Time-bound (SMART). This framework ensures that your goals are clear, realistic, and trackable. You'll learn how to create growth goals that challenge you while being aligned with your values and overall self-love journey.

- **Creating a personal growth plan**: Goal-setting is most effective when it is accompanied by a solid plan. This section will help you develop a personalized growth plan that includes actionable steps for reaching your goals, along with timelines and milestones to track your progress. You'll also learn how to maintain flexibility, adjusting your plan as needed while staying committed to your personal development.

- **Celebrating your progress**: A key aspect of self-love is recognizing and celebrating your achievements, no matter how small. This section will emphasize the importance of acknowledging your growth, staying motivated, and enjoying the journey toward personal development.

Setting and pursuing personal growth goals that are rooted in self-love allows you to lead a life that is continuously evolving and aligned with your true self. Through thoughtful goal-setting, you nurture your personal growth while honoring your needs and aspirations.

14.3 Embracing Change and Adapting to Growth

Change is a natural part of personal growth, and learning to embrace it is essential for maintaining self-love. Growth often involves stepping outside of your comfort zone and navigating uncertainties, but self-love provides the emotional resilience needed to adapt and thrive through these changes.

Let us look at these points:

Why embracing change is key to self-love and growth: Change can be challenging, but resisting it can hinder your personal development. This section will explore why embracing change is necessary for self-love, as it allows you to evolve and become the best version of yourself. When you love yourself, you're more willing to let go of what no longer serves you and welcome new opportunities that support your growth.

- **Strategies for adapting to change**: Adapting to change requires resilience, flexibility, and a positive mindset. This section will offer practical strategies for coping with the uncertainties that come with growth, such as reframing challenges as opportunities, practicing mindfulness, and staying focused on your long-term goals. You'll learn how to stay grounded during times of transition, using self-love as a guiding force.

- **Building resilience through self-love**: Resilience is the ability to bounce back from setbacks and keep moving forward. Self-love plays a crucial role in building resilience, as it helps you maintain confidence and inner strength during difficult times. This section will provide tools for strengthening your resilience, including self-compassion, self-care, and a growth-oriented mindset.
- **Staying focused on your self-love goals**: Growth is a continuous process, and staying focused on your self-love goals requires dedication and perseverance. This section will offer tips for staying motivated, tracking your progress, and adjusting your

approach as you grow. By remaining committed to your self-love journey, you ensure that your personal development is sustainable and fulfilling.

By embracing change and adapting to growth, you cultivate a deeper sense of self-love and unlock your potential for ongoing personal development. Change becomes a positive force in your life, guiding you toward greater fulfillment and self-awareness.

In Conclusion

As we come to the end of this book, it's important to recognize that self-love is a lifelong journey. It is not a destination, but a continuous practice of nurturing and honoring yourself in all aspects of your life, emotionally, mentally, physically, and spiritually.

Recap of Key Principles and Practices:

- **Self-love as the foundation**: Throughout this book, you've learned that self-love is the foundation for a fulfilling and authentic life. By prioritizing self-care, setting boundaries, and pursuing your passions, you create a life that reflects your true self.

- **Embracing growth**: Personal growth is an integral part of the self-love journey. You've explored how self-love fosters a growth mindset, encourages resilience, and empowers you to embrace change.

- **Integrating self-love into all areas of life**: From relationships to career and personal development, self-love is the guiding principle that enhances every aspect of your existence.

As you move forward, continue to practice self-love daily. Be patient with yourself, celebrate your progress, and embrace the challenges and growth that lie ahead. By committing to your self-love journey, you will continue to evolve into the best version of yourself.

Thank you for embarking on this journey toward self-love. May you continue to nurture and cherish yourself, embracing all that you are and all that you aspire to be.

Epilogue: The Journey Continues

As you close the final chapter of this book, I want to remind you of one important truth: self-love is not a destination but a lifelong journey. It is a practice, a commitment to yourself that requires patience, compassion, and perseverance. Throughout this book, we've explored the foundational concepts of self-love, tackled negative self-talk, embraced our authentic selves, and discussed practical strategies to build healthier boundaries, relationships, and routines. But the work doesn't stop here.

What you've learned is not meant to be left on these pages. Each chapter was crafted to guide you toward actionable change, but it is up to you to apply these principles to your daily life. The affirmations you speak, the boundaries you set, and the care you extend toward yourself are all part of this ongoing practice of self-love. It's important to remember that there will be setbacks and days when practicing self-love feels difficult. On those days, remind yourself of the progress you've made and the tools you now have at your disposal.

In the same way that this book was inspired by personal growth and the wisdom of others, your journey of self-love will inspire those around you. As you nurture self-compassion, authenticity, and a commitment to your well-being, you'll find that your inner light grows brighter and that light will inevitably touch others. By loving yourself fully, you contribute to creating a more compassionate and positive world.

So, as this book comes to an end, let this not be the end of your journey but a renewed beginning. Go forward with confidence, knowing that you have the tools, insights, and strength to cultivate self-love in every aspect of your life. Continue exploring, growing, and, most importantly, loving yourself deeply. This journey is yours to own, embrace it fully.

Thank you for allowing me to walk alongside you on this path. The adventure of self-love is just beginning, and I believe the best is yet to come.

With love and gratitude,
Yemisi Daniels

Made in the USA
Columbia, SC
22 November 2024

46703039R00083